Contents

KU-520-233

Welcome to Hollywood!

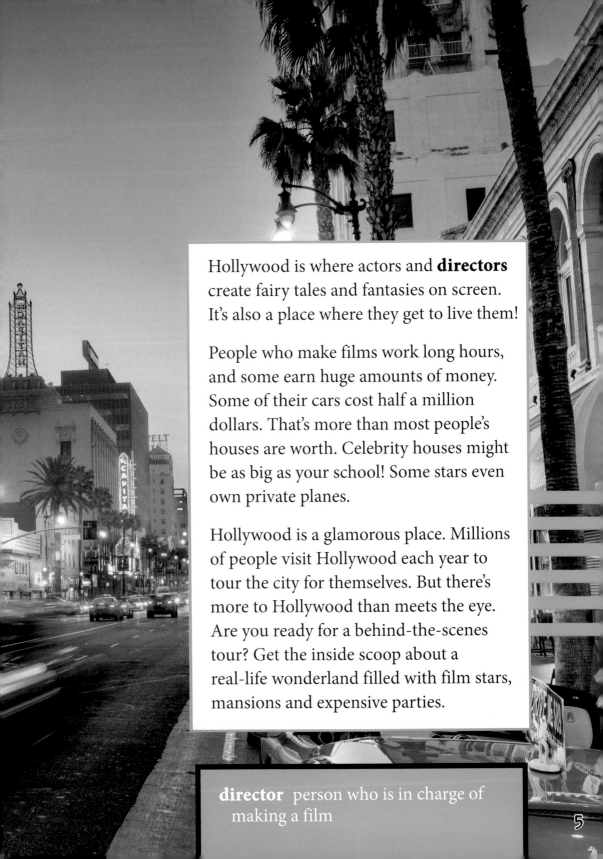

Hollywood is where actors and **directors** create fairy tales and fantasies on screen. It's also a place where they get to live them!

People who make films work long hours, and some earn huge amounts of money. Some of their cars cost half a million dollars. That's more than most people's houses are worth. Celebrity houses might be as big as your school! Some stars even own private planes.

Hollywood is a glamorous place. Millions of people visit Hollywood each year to tour the city for themselves. But there's more to Hollywood than meets the eye. Are you ready for a behind-the-scenes tour? Get the inside scoop about a real-life wonderland filled with film stars, mansions and expensive parties.

director person who is in charge of making a film

CHAPTER 1

Hollywood history

"Hollywood" refers to an area in Los Angeles, California, USA, where films are made. But it can also describe the film business itself. The business of film-making has been around for about 125 years. It's gone through a lot of changes in that time.

In the early 1900s, the first films looked very different from the ones made today. They were made in black and white instead of colour. Each film was only a few minutes long. They didn't even have sound! They were called silent films.

Early films weren't made in Hollywood. Most were made in France, New York City and New Jersey. But it's hard to make films year-round in places that have snowy winters. Film-makers soon started moving out to sunny Los Angeles. **Producers** made the first Hollywood film in 1910. Before long, many others followed.

Los Angeles is Spanish for "The Angels". That's easier to say than the city's original name. It was *El Pueblo de Nuestra Señora la Reina de los Ángeles del Río Porciúncula*. That means "Town of Our Lady the Queen of Angels of the River Porciúncula". The name was shortened in the early 1800s.

You may already know that Thomas Edison helped mass produce the light bulb. Did you know he had a part in inventing America's first film camera too? Edison and William Dickson invented what they called the Kinetograph. Edison also built the USA's first film **studio** near his home in New Jersey.

producer person who puts the many parts of a film together

studio place where films and television and radio programmes are made

How will you know when you arrive in Hollywood?
There's a giant sign to tell you. Each letter is about
14 metres (45 feet) tall and 10 metres (33 feet) wide.
The whole sign weighs about 218,000 kg (480,000 pounds).
That's as heavy as 20 single-decker buses!

HOLLYWOODLAND

When the Hollywood sign was put up in 1923, it said
"Hollywoodland". About 20 years later, the sign was in a
terrible state and needed to be replaced. By then, people
around the world knew it as "Hollywood". A replacement
sign was made in 1949 that just said "Hollywood".

In 1953 a group of businessmen wanted to honour the celebrities who were making Hollywood famous. Five years later, they began adding stars to the pavement on Hollywood Boulevard. Each star represented a popular entertainer. Today more than 2,600 stars cover 15 pavements. This is called the Hollywood Walk of Fame. You'll find everyone from Walt Disney to Scarlett Johansson represented there. There are even stars for Snoopy, Shrek and Godzilla!

It's a great honour to be invited to have a star on the Walk of Fame. But celebrities have to pay for them. And at $30,000 each, they don't come cheap!

show me the money

When the first permanent cinema in the United States opened in 1905, a ticket cost only a nickel (3p). Today tickets in the US cost about $9 (£6). That's almost 200 times more! And that's not the only thing that's gone up...

In 1938 Judy Garland earned $500 a week to play Dorothy in *The Wizard of Oz*. The dog who played her pet, Toto, earned $125 a week!

In 2011 Johnny Depp was paid $55 million to play Captain Jack Sparrow in *Pirates of the Caribbean: On Stranger Tides*. The film broke a record for the most expensive Hollywood film ever. It cost $410.6 million to make. But it earned more than $1 billion!

As of 2018, six **animated** films had also made more than $1 billion each. How many of them have you seen?

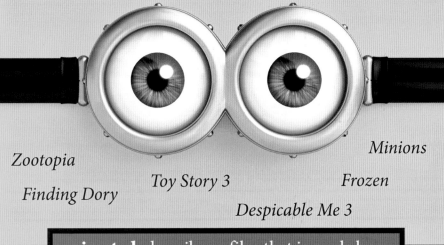

Zootopia

Minions

Toy Story 3

Frozen

Finding Dory

Despicable Me 3

animated describes a film that is made by projecting a series of drawings very quickly, one after the other, so that the characters in the drawings seem to move

In 1977, director George Lucas was sure his original *Star Wars* film was going to flop. Embarrassed, Lucas went on holiday to Hawaii when the film was released. No one was more surprised than he was when *Star Wars* earned more than $300 million in cinemas. At the time, that was more than any other film had ever made.

Hollywood is packed with expensive, over-the-top mansions. Reality TV star Kim Kardashian and hip-hop artist Kanye West shared an $11 million house. It had a bowling alley, a cinema and a basketball court. There was a giant garage for Kim's $325,000 Ferrari and Kanye's $440,000 Lamborghini. They even had $750,000 gold-plated toilets. The couple sold the home in 2017 for $17.8 million.

Daniel Radcliffe made more than $70 million for playing Harry Potter in all eight films. He's tried to save most of his money. But he did once spend $17,000 on a mattress.

Hogwarts

Actor Nicolas Cage is a pretty big spender. His film credits go back almost 40 years. While some celebrities buy mansions, Cage owned two castles. He also had two islands, a pet octopus and a comic book worth $150,000! At one point Cage almost went bankrupt.

CHAPTER 3

Film magic

Hundreds of people work on a film before it gets to cinemas. Take a look at some of the secrets you won't see on screen.

Every film is put together **scene** by scene. In 1931 actor and director Charlie Chaplin made his popular comedy *City Lights*. He reshot one scene 342 times.

scene part of a story, play or film that shows what is happening in one place and time

Many films are set in one city, but filmed in another. The 2016 remake of *Ghostbusters* is set in New York. That film was actually filmed in Boston, Massachusetts. *Spider-Man: Homecoming* is supposed to take place in New York City. It was actually shot in Atlanta, Georgia, and Los Angeles, California. Iceland is often used to represent outer space. Parts of *Star Trek: Into Darkness*, *Star Wars: The Force Awakens* and *Rogue One: A Star Wars Story* were all filmed there.

Next time you watch an action film, pay close attention to the lead actor or actress. If you can't see his or her face, it might be because someone else is playing the part. Stunt people take over when a scene is dangerous. They're trained to race cars or jump off buildings. They don't get the fame, but they do get to do the coolest stuff!

Some actors do their own stunts, but it can be risky! Jackie Chan does all of his dangerous fight scenes. He's broken his skull, most of his fingers, his ankle and his cheekbone. He's also broken his nose four times.

Films have shown space fights, dragons and hurricanes. How do film-makers create such scenes? Today, they use **computer-generated imagery (CGI)**. These special effects are added by computers after a film has been made. Take Iron Man's awesome armour, for example. During filming, actor Robert Downey Jr was usually just wearing a tight red bodysuit. Then it was transformed into armour by CGI.

computer-generated imagery (CGI) way to make special effects using a computer

Actor Andy Serkis specializes in CGI-based characters. For these roles he does all his acting in a special suit. It covers his body with sensors that record his movements. Once a scene has been filmed, CGI animation can transform the way he looks. That's how he was able to play the creepy creature Gollum in the *Lord of the Rings* and *Hobbit* films. It's also how he became the title character in *King Kong* and the ape leader in *Planet of the Apes*. He also played Supreme Leader Snoke in the *Star Wars* films.

Most films with special effects also use green screens. These look like plain green backgrounds while a film is being made. When you watch characters running away from spaceships or villains, they're probably inside a studio. Or they might be on an empty city street. And they're running from . . . nothing! Backgrounds are added in later.

In films, things aren't always what they appear to be. When you see Hogwarts school in a Harry Potter film, you're often looking at a model that's about 15 metres (50 feet) wide. The whole thing fits inside a single room! The beds that Harry and his best friend, Ron, use are tiny. By the end of the series, the actors' legs were hanging off the ends of the beds. The film-makers left that part off screen.

Special effects also include
sounds. In *Jurassic Park*
the sounds of angry
dinosaurs are actually
horses, geese
and baby elephants.

Make-up goes a long way towards creating a fantasy.
It took make-up artists five hours every morning to
turn Dave Bautista into the alien warrior Drax for
Guardians of the Galaxy. It took another hour and a
half to take off all his make-up at the end of each day.

super celebrations

Hollywood is a party place! Every week there are celebrations, from **premieres** to **wrap** parties and awards shows. These events are great excuses for actors to put on expensive suits and designer dresses!

premiere first public performance of a film, play or work of music or dance

wrap completed filming

GROWN UPS
IN THEATERS JUNE 25

Films take months to make and involve hundreds of people. When filming has finished, the cast and **crew** have a big party. They may give each other "wrap gifts". After Adam Sandler made the comedy *Grown Ups*, he gave his castmates new cars!

crew team of people who work together behind the scenes to produce a film

When a film is ready for the public to see, film-makers throw a premiere party. Big premiere parties can cost millions of dollars. One of the most expensive premieres in history was for *Pearl Harbor*. Two thousand people attended the $5 million party. It was held on a naval ship in Hawaii. The event included nearly $1 million worth of fireworks!

The most important night in Hollywood is the Academy Awards. The event is also called the Oscars. This event gives awards to the people who made the best films of the year. The first Oscars was held in 1929. That ceremony lasted 15 minutes and was attended by 270 people. Now it costs about $40 million to plan the event. Around 3,400 people pack the theatre, and more than 30 million others watch the awards on TV.

Many people have won more than one Oscar. But so far Walt Disney has the most. By the end of his career, he'd won 22 awards.

Tatum O'Neal was the youngest actor to win an Oscar. She was just 10 when she earned the Academy Award for Best Supporting Actress. She played Addie Loggins in the 1973 film *Paper Moon*. Her real dad, Ryan O'Neal, played her father in the film.

The Academy Awards ceremony is Hollywood's most glamorous event of the year. But the funniest is probably the Golden Raspberry Awards. At this ceremony trophies called Razzies are given to actors of the year's worst films. Sandra Bullock once won an Oscar and a Razzie in the same weekend for two different films. The Razzie was for a comedy called *All About Steve*. The Oscar was for a drama called *The Blind Side*.

The money that goes into an actor's wardrobe at the Academy Awards can be mind-blowing. Nicole Kidman once wore a necklace worth $7 million to the Oscars. It had 7,500 diamonds in it and took more than 6,000 hours to make!

At the 2013 Oscars, Jennifer Lawrence wore a gown worth $4 million. Unfortunately, the dress was too long. When she went on stage to accept her award, she tripped!

A **nomination** for an Academy Award is a huge honour. It also comes with gift bags. Past gifts have included diamond jewellery, bicycles and surfing lessons. Other gifts have included trips to Hawaii, Italy and Japan.

nominate name someone as a candidate for an award

After the Oscars are over, the guests go to the biggest party of the year. It's called the Governor's Ball. Hundreds of chefs work for weeks to prepare the food. Past menus have included soup with real gold flakes and corn dogs stuffed with lobster. A dessert buffet table spans the entire room. It's filled with sweets from caramel lollipops to 7,000 mini chocolate Oscar statues.

star surprises

You see Hollywood's biggest stars in your favourite films and TV series. Sometimes it may feel like you know them. But there's still a lot more to learn. Remember these fun facts the next time you see these celebrities on screen.

Hugh Jackman

Gal Gadot

Actors usually have other jobs before they get into the film business. Hugh Jackman became very famous after playing Wolverine in the *X-Men* films. But he used to work as a PE teacher and a party clown. Israeli actress Gal Gadot was a soldier in the army before she became an actress and starred in films such as *Wonder Woman*.

Actors move to Hollywood because that's where they work. But many grew up far from LA. Hugh Jackman, Nicole Kidman and Naomi Watts are Australian. Charlize Theron is from South Africa. Ryan Gosling, Rachel McAdams and Jim Carrey are Canadian. Amy Adams was born in Italy. Emma Watson was born in Paris, France.

Some actors may not have seemed like the perfect fit for their roles. Johnny Depp played Willy Wonka in *Charlie and the Chocolate Factory*. In real life, he was allergic to chocolate when he was a child. Luckily, he outgrew his allergy. James Earl Jones is known for being the voice of *Star Wars* villain Darth Vader. But he stuttered so badly as a child that he barely spoke.

Stars don't just spend their money on fast cars and huge houses. Many of them work hard to make the world a better place. Oscar-winning actor Leonardo DiCaprio has his own charity. He is especially dedicated to helping animals and the environment. The Leonardo DiCaprio Foundation works to protect oceans, forests and other habitats against climate change.

Harrison Ford is famous for playing *Star Wars* pilot Han Solo. But he's a pilot in real life, too. Ford owns several planes, which he uses to help people in need. He even flew supplies to Haiti after the country had a terrible earthquake in 2010.

HAITI

Dominican Republic

Some stars get tired of the Hollywood life. They happily give up fame to do something else. Peter Ostrum played Charlie in the 1971 film *Willy Wonka & the Chocolate Factory*. Then he decided acting wasn't for him. He grew up to become a vet instead.

Does Hollywood sound like somewhere you'd like to live? It's a crazy place with weird and wonderful surprises around every corner. And now that you know some of the secrets behind the scenes, you may never look at films the same way again!

Glossary

animated describes a film that is made by projecting a series of drawings very quickly, one after the other, so that the characters in the drawings seem to move

computer-generated imagery way to make special effects using a computer; also called CGI

crew team of people who work together behind the scenes to produce a film or TV series

director person who is in charge of making a film

nominate name someone as a candidate for an award

premiere first public performance of a film, play or work of music or dance

producer person who puts the many parts of a film together

scene part of a story, play or film that shows what is happening in one place and time

studio place where films and television and radio programmes are made

wrap completed filming

Find out more

Books

Children's Book of Cinema, DK (DK Children, 2014)

Scarlett Johansson (Hollywood Action Heroes), Peter Delmar (Raintree, 2016)

Special Effects Make-Up Artist (The Coolest Jobs on the Planet), Jonathan Craig and Bridget Light (Raintree, 2014)

Websites

www.bbc.co.uk/schools/gcsebitesize/english/creativewriting/ movingimagesrev6.shtml
Learn more about the language that film-makers use.

www.leonardodicaprio.org
Learn more about the work being done by Leonardo DiCaprio's foundation.

Index